ANCIENT EGYPT

Anne Millard

Illustrated by Joseph McEwan
and Roger Mann

Designed by Kim Blundell
Edited by Jane Chisholm

Contents

Printed in Spain by
GRAFICAS REUNIDAS, S. A.
Av. de Aragón, 56 — Madrid-27.

First published in 1981 by
Usborne Publishing Ltd,
20 Garrick Street, London WC2E 9EJ,
England.

Published in Australia by
Rigby Publishing Ltd,
Adelaide, Sydney, Melbourne, Brisbane

About this Book

This pocket guide is full of fascinating information and colourful pictures which will bring to life the world of the Ancient Egyptians. There are lots of scenes, like the one above of people working in the fields, which have been carefully reconstructed from archaeological evidence.

Sometimes, instead of a reconstructed scene, you will see a reproduction of an Egyptian painting or carving – like this one of musicians playing. You will usually be able to recognize these by the flat way in which the figures are drawn. Also, the Egyptians always drew faces sideways on.

You will also find reproductions of models the Egyptians made and detailed pictures of things they used, such as furniture, jewellery, tools or weapons. Some are based on objects shown in Egyptian paintings or sculpture, but most of them show objects that have survived in tombs and still exist today.

The map on page 58 shows you where many of the places are that are mentioned in the book.

Sometimes you will read about people other than Egyptians – Nubians or Syrians, for example. You can find out where they come from by looking at the map on page 4.

Your can find out more about the kings and queens mentioned in the book by looking at the "History of Ancient Egypt" on pages 59-61. Egypt's long history is divided into "Kingdoms" and "Periods", and you will come across these terms in the book. To find out more about them, see page 5.

You may want to visit a museum to see some Ancient Egyptian objects yourself. On page 62 there is a list of museums with good Egyptian collections.

Introduction to Ancient Egypt

The civilization of Ancient Egypt is one of the oldest in the world. It began more than 5,000 years ago and lasted for over 3,000 years. For a time Egypt was divided into two kingdoms – Upper and Lower Egypt. Then, in 3118BC*, the country was united and ruled by one king, called the pharaoh.

This book is mainly concerned with Egypt between 3118 and 30BC. During this time the Egyptians conquered many foreign lands and acquired an empire.

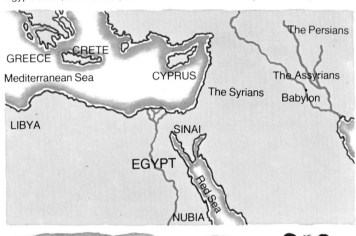

Thousands of years ago, the Sahara was green and fertile and inhabited by Stone Age hunters. Gradually the climate changed and the land became a desert. The hunters left to search for new land and settled in Egypt. There they learnt how to tame animals and plant seeds and became farmers. People may also have come from the south and east.

The Ancient Egyptians were descended from these early hunters. At the peak of their civilization they produced great works of art, such as this mask of King Tutankhamum. Religion and the idea of life after death played a very important part in their lives.

In 30BC the Romans invaded. Egypt became a province of the Roman Empire and ceased to be an independent nation.

*3118BC means 3118 years before Christ.

Later the Egyptians became Christians, and then Muslims, and the ancient temples and palaces were buried in the sand and forgotten. In the 18th century, European travellers became interested in the ruins and then professional archaeologists began to dig. The hot, dry climate had helped to preserve things.

Much of what we know about the Egyptians comes from tombs. They believed the afterlife would be like life on earth, so they put in their tombs the things they thought they would need, such as food and furniture.

They painted the insides of the tombs with scenes from daily life, such as grape picking. These pictures tell us a lot about their lives. Also found in tombs were models which show people doing things and scrolls with writing on them. Some of it was a kind of picture writing we call hieroglyphics.

At that time, nobody knew how to read hieroglyphics. However, in 1799, a clue was found. A stone was dug up in the Nile Delta with three kinds of writing on it – Greek and two kinds of Egyptian, including hieroglyphics. A French scholar called Champollion worked out the meaning of one word by comparing the Greek with the hieroglyphs. From this word he was able to break the code and the Egyptian scrolls and inscriptions could be read.

This chart shows you the terms that are used for the different periods of Egyptian history. The important periods are the Old, Middle and New Kingdoms. The kings have been divided into "Dynasties", which are families or branches of families. This was done in the 3rd century BC, by an Egyptian priest called Manetho, who wrote a history of Ancient Egypt.

Period	Date	Dynasties
Predynastic	–3118BC	
Archaic	3118–2686BC	1 & 2
Old Kingdom	2686–2181BC	3–6
1st Intermediate Period	2181-2040BC	7–10
Middle Kingdom	2040-1786BC	11 & 12
2nd Intermediate Period	1786–1567BC	13–17
New Kingdom	1567–1085BC	18–20
3rd Intermediate Period	1085–664BC	21–25
Late Period	664–332BC	26–30
Ptolemaic Period	332–30BC	31

Life in the Country

Egypt is a hot, dry country with very little rain. Crops can only be grown in the lush, green fields along the banks of the River Nile, which was where nearly everyone lived.

The Ancient Egyptians pictured the Nile as a generous god called Hapy (shown here), who gave life and food to the land and the people.

Every July, the Nile flooded the land for a few weeks. This was called the "Inundation". The mud left behind made rich, fertile soil.

"Nilometres" were built to measure the height of the flood, so people could work out if there was enough water to provide a good harvest.

When there was not enough water for the crops, people starved. This carving shows people starving during a bad year.

To avoid the floods, the Egyptians built their villages on high ground or dug ditches round them to drain off the water.

To make use of the flood water, large canals were built, with a series of connecting channels and ditches to take the water to all parts of the fields.

Farmers controlled the flow of water to their crops by opening and closing the channels each day. It was a serious crime to try to cut off somebody else's supply.

The boundaries of the fields were marked with stones. Occasionally a dishonest farmer would try to steal some of his neighbour's land by moving the stones during the flood.

The king was in charge of making sure the vital water supply kept flowing. Here the king is opening a new canal.

People spent a few weeks every year working on the canals to keep them in good repair. This was part of a tax they owed to the king.

This figure is called a shabti. Shabtis were put in tombs to do the canal digging for the dead person in the afterlife.

A shaduf is a bucket hung from a beam, with a weight at the other end. The Egyptians used them to raise water from the Nile into the canals. They are still used in Egypt today.

Water was carried from place to place in jars hanging from a yoke. These people are carrying water to water the lettuces in their vegetable garden.

A farmhouse

This house belongs to a wealthy farmer. We know what the houses looked like from pottery models, called "soul houses", which were put in people's tombs.

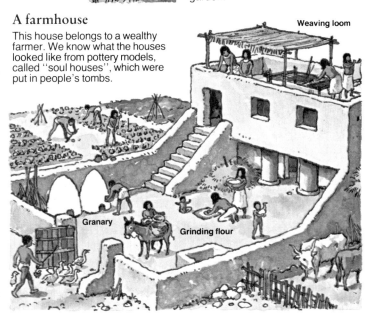

Weaving loom

Granary

Grinding flour

Sowing and Harvesting

In October, as the floods went down, farmers began to plough their fields. They used ploughs made of wood and bronze.

The main crops were wheat and barley. The seeds were sown by hand and animals were driven over the fields to tread them into the soil.

Animal skins filled with water were hung in the trees so that thirsty workers could refresh themselves.

As the crops grew, there was weeding and watering to be done and throwing stones to scare away the birds.

Then the taxman arrived. Here a worried farmer and his wife greet him with gifts, hoping for special treatment.

The taxman and his helpers measured the crops in the fields, to work out how much would be harvested and the amount that should be paid to the king in taxes.

Many things could go wrong before harvest time. The crop could be stolen or destroyed, but the farmer still had to pay the full amount of tax.

The harvest

The harvest was in March and April. Men cut the wheat using sickles with flint blades. People behind them gathered it together and loaded it into panniers, to be taken home on the backs of donkeys.

Women brought food and beer to the hungry harvesters. They also did the gleaning – collecting the wheat the men had missed.

Carvings in tombs show that musicians were hired to play to encourage the harvesters to work hard.

Offerings were put in the fields for the harvest goddess, Renenutet, who appeared as a snake to protect the grain.

In order to thresh the wheat (separate the grain from the straw), it was trampled on by cattle, which were driven round and round an area called a threshing floor.

To separate the grain from the chaff (its outer cover), women tossed it into the air, so the light chaff blew away. This process is called ''winnowing''.

Most people couldn't write, so scribes* were employed to record how well the harvest was going and what the yield was.

Granaries were for storing grain. The grain was poured through a hole in the roof and taken out through doors at the bottom.

The Egyptians did not use money, so farmers gave some of their crops or animals as taxes to the king.

Anyone who did not pay his taxes would be beaten as a punishment.

When the floods came, many people went off to work for the king. This was another way of paying tax.

*For more about scribes, see page 52

9

Houses

The earliest houses archaeologists have found in Egypt were round huts made of reeds.

By the Middle Kingdom houses were built of sun-dried mud bricks and were rectangular. This model is from the 1st Intermediate Period.

This is a painting of a New Kingdom house. It looks a bit strange because the Egyptians didn't use perspective in their drawing.

A villa at Tell el Amarna

Many Ancient Egyptian sites have towns built on them now, so it is difficult to find houses to excavate. Amarna is an exception as no-one lives there now. This is a rich man's villa built in the New Kingdom. It is made of mud brick with a wooden roof and columns. It has a second storey which covers only part of the building. The front and centre of the house are used for conducting business and entertaining friends. The back of the house is where the family sleeps. Sometimes in the summer they sleep on the roof.

Stables

K

Rich people had bathrooms and lavatories in their houses. The walls were lined with stone to stop water splashing the bricks.

Often the walls were painted bright colours or had mats hung on them. This is part of a painted leather wall-hanging.

This is part of the painted mud floor of a villa. The rich sometimes had floors covered with glazed tiles.

Servants' quarters

Granaries for storing grain

Windows – they are small and high because of the heat.

Furniture

Most Egyptian houses had less furniture than ours. It was usually made from plain wood and reed, but rich people had furniture made from rare woods, inlaid with ivory or semi-precious stones and covered with gold. Some furniture had designs on it of flowers, animals or hieroglyphs.*

Thrones

These are the thrones of Queen Hetepheres (left) and King Tutankhamun (right). They are made of wood and covered with real gold.

Chairs

Most chairs had short legs and no arms. The legs were often carved to look like animals' legs.

Stools and cushions

Many people had stools, rather than chairs, or sat on cushions on the floor.

Inside a scribe's house

This is what it would have looked like inside the house of a scribe, who would have been fairly rich. The furniture is well-made but doesn't have the decorated inlays that a king's or noble's furniture would have had. There are mats, and curtains on the door made of reeds.

A princess's bedroom

The bed is made up with linen sheets. There is a wooden head-rest on the bed, which the Egyptians used instead of a pillow. The princess's clothes, wigs, jewels and make-up are all kept in boxes, inlaid with gold, ivory, semi-precious stones or faience – a substance rather like glazed china. The floors and walls are painted.

Chests and boxes

Chests, boxes and baskets of various shapes and sizes were common in every household. People used them for storing clothes and other things, as there were no cupboards.

Lamps

For lights, the Egyptians used lamps, which burned linseed oil. They varied from simple clay (left) to alabaster (right).

Tables

Tables, like chairs, usually had quite short legs.

Pot stands

Many Egyptian pots and jars had rounded or pointed bases. Stands made of wood or clay were used to keep them upright.

Clothes

The clothes of the Ancient Egyptians were made of linen, which comes from a plant called flax. In winter though, some people wore wool. Although fashions changed among the rich, most people's clothes remained much the same throughout the whole period.

A man wore a short kilt and a woman wore an ankle length tunic with two shoulder straps.

For much of the year it was very hot, so children often did not wear clothes at all.

For heavy outdoor work men usually wore loincloths, and women wore short skirts.

Headcloths were sometimes worn, but most people went bare-headed.

In winter it could get quite cold, so people wrapped themselves in large cloaks.

Everyone wore sandals made of leather or reed. Some nobles' sandals were made in quite fancy styles.

Some clothes, such as this linen robe, have been found in tombs. The gloves came from Tutankhamun's tomb, but there are no paintings showing people wearing gloves.

Making cloth

The flax to make the cloth is grown in fields. First it was picked, then the stems were washed and separated.

Pieces of stem were twisted together into a long, strong thread. This process is called spinning.

To make the cloth, the threads were woven on a loom. This job was done by women.

14

Old Kingdom

These are the clothes that would have been worn by nobles in the Old Kingdom. The woman is wearing a dress of beads over a plain white dress. The man's kilt is partly pleated.

Young men preferred their kilts short. Elderly officials wore much longer ones.

Middle Kingdom

This is a Middle Kingdom official and his wife. She is wearing a dress with embroidery on it.

Materials

The clothes shown in tomb paintings are usually white, as white was thought to be pure. However, small pieces of cloth and statues have been found, which show that the Egyptians did use coloured and patterned materials.

New Kingdom

In the New Kingdom, the clothes worn by the rich became much more elaborate. Women wore finely pleated dresses and flowing cloaks. Men sometimes wore long robes over their kilts.

Feathers and sequins

Some statues show kings and queens wearing clothes made of feathers. This picture shows a section of one of the statues.

Lots of rosettes and sequins have been found in Tutankhamun's tomb. They were probably sewn on to clothes.

Hair and Make-up

Egyptian men and women, of all ages and social backgrounds, used make-up. They kept it in boxes or baskets, like these.

The rich had mirrors made from highly polished silver, with decorated wooden handles. Poorer people had mirrors made of copper instead.

Palette
Oil
Jar
Powder

Lip and eye paints were made from minerals which were finely ground into powder on a palette. The powder was stored in jars and then mixed with oil or water before use.

Make-up was painted on to the eyes and lips with fine brushes and sticks.

People painted their eyelids with a green or grey paint, called kohl. They shaped their eyebrows with tweezers.

Razors were used for shaving hair. Priests kept their heads and bodies shaved.

This statue of a dancer has tattoos on its legs and arms. Some mummies have been found with tattoos.

Perfume

This carving shows women gathering lilies for perfume. The Egyptians made a lot of perfume, from flowers and scented wood.

The flowers were then mixed with oil or fat and left in pots, until the oil had absorbed the scent.

Perfumed oils were rubbed into the skin, to stop it from drying in the hot Egyptian sun.

Hairstyles

As the climate was very hot, most men and women kept their hair short, especially if they had to work outdoors.

Nobles had longer hair or wore wigs. Some kept their hair straight, others had plaits or curls.

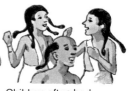

Children often had shaved heads with a single lock of hair. Young girls sometimes had several plaits.

The hairstyles of nobles varied according to the period. These are the styles worn in the Old Kingdom.

In the Middle Kingdom noblewomen sometimes wore their hair padded out and decorated with ornaments.

New Kingdom styles were very elaborate. For special occasions nobles wore heavy wigs with a lot of plaits and curls.

Wigs and combs have been found in tombs. The wigs were made of wool or real hair.

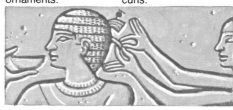

Instead of a full wig, some women added individual locks of false hair to their own. This carving shows a maid attaching a lock to her mistress's hair.

Both men and women wore perfume. They kept it in flasks like these.

This painting of a banquet shows a servant putting cones of perfumed grease on the heads of the guests. As the grease melted, it ran down the face with a pleasant, cooling effect.

Jewellery

Egypt and Nubia had gold mines, so a lot of jewellery was made of gold. This is an ancient map of a mine.

After being mined, the gold was weighed at every stage to make sure none of it had been stolen.

Goldsmiths heated the gold until it melted. To keep the fire hot, they pumped bellows with their feet.

The melted gold was then poured into moulds, or left to set and hammered into shape when it was cold.

The Egyptians used semi-precious stones, such as turquoise, garnet and lapis lazuli. Here, stones are being threaded into a necklace.

There was a wide range of jewellery for both men and women, though tomb paintings always show people wearing the same styles.

Crowns and head-dresses

Head-dress

Diadem

Rich people often wore some sort of jewelled head-dress. Here is a princess's diadem and a head-dress that was worn in the New Kingdom.

These delicate diadems belonged to a 12th Dynasty princess.

Here is an elaborate head-dress, worn by one of the minor wives of King Tuthmosis III.

Gold headbands and hair ornaments, like these, were worn by many noblewomen.

Earrings

Earrings were fashionable in the New Kingdom. Men and women had pierced ears.

Rings

People of all classes wore rings. Some had seals on them, or charms, called amulets.

Necklaces

Pendants were made in all kinds of materials, from shell to silver, which was rare and more expensive than gold.

Strings of beads were very common, judging from the number that have been found in tombs.

This bead collar is typical of the kind worn in the New Kingdom. It was fastened by cords at the back of the neck.

Pectorals

A pectoral was a large piece of jewellery, made in the form of a picture. It was hung around the neck on a string of beads.

This vulture pectoral belonged to King Tutankhamun. The vulture represents the goddess Mut, who was supposed to protect the king.

The decoration on this pectoral includes a scarab beetle and the eye of the god Horus. They are amulets, or charms which were designed to ward off evil spirits.

Belts

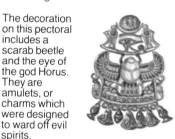

These dancing girls are wearing belts made of beads, some of which are shaped like shells. The beads are hollow inside and contain grains of metal that jingle as they move.

Funerary jewels

Most people had their jewels buried with them. Some, like these pottery beads, were made specially to be put in a tomb.

Bracelets and armlets

Men and women both wore bracelets and armlets. They could be a single string of beads, or a broad band of metal or beads.

Anklets

A lot of Egyptian women wore anklets, except when they were working.

Food

The Egyptians grew grapes for eating as a fruit and for making wine. They were grown on trellises like this.

Baboons were sometimes trained to pick figs for their owners, though the ones in this painting seem to be eating the fruit themselves.

Here are some of the fruit and vegetables grown in Ancient Egypt – cucumbers, peas, lettuces, onions, garlic, dates and pomegranates.

The Egyptians used honey to sweeten their food. Bees were kept in pottery jars.

The god Min looked after crops and animals. This carving shows the king making an offering to him.

Birds

Most farmers kept geese and ducks. This painting of geese is from an Old Kingdom tomb.

On some large farms, birds, such as pigeons and storks, were raised in aviaries and fattened for eating.

Catching wild fowl

The reeds along the River Nile teemed with wild ducks and other water birds. Fowlers trapped the birds with huge nets and sold them at the market. They were caught for eating, not just as a sport.

Animals

There was little land for grazing, as most fertile land was needed for growing crops. Egyptian cows were small.

When the floods came, herdsmen had to lead their cattle to the safety of higher ground.

A lot of cows were kept for milking. As milk goes sour quickly in hot climates, most of it was made into cheese.

Only rich people could afford to eat a lot of beef. Cattle for eating were kept in sheds and specially fattened up.

Sheep were raised for mutton. There were two kinds of sheep – one had horizontal horns, the other, curled ones.

The Egyptians kept goats for their milk and meat.

Pigs were kept, though they were associated with the wicked god, Set, so priests never ate pork.

For a time, people tried keeping hyenas to eat, but soon gave it up. The hyenas were probably too dangerous or too tough to eat.

The painting shows produce from the desert. Animals, such as deer, were hunted for meat; ostriches, for their eggs and feathers.

Fishing

The Egyptians ate a lot of fish. Fishermen usually went out in boats with huge nets. Sometimes two boats drifted side by side with a net between them. Some fishermen fished on their own, catching fish from the bank, using small nets or lines and hooks.

21

Cooking

Here are some butchers at work. Cattle were roped and pulled on to their sides to be slaughtered. The meat was then cut into joints and hung, ready to be eaten.

The Egyptians ate both wild and domesticated birds. After their necks were wrung, the birds were plucked and cleaned.

Here, fish are being gutted and cleaned. Sometimes fish was cooked and eaten immediately, but it could also be dried and stored.

Here is an Egyptian whisk and strainer made of reeds. Sometimes cooking utensils were put in tombs, to be used in the afterlife.

Most cooking was done outdoors away from the house, to avoid the danger of it catching fire. Sticks and dried grass were used as fuel.

To start the fire, a bow string was twisted round a stick and rubbed hard until it produced sparks.

Meat was often grilled over a brazier like this. A fan was used to keep the fire burning properly.

Making bread

Bread was an important part of the Egyptians' diet. Flour was made by grinding wheat or barley between two stones.

The flour was then mixed with water to make dough. Sometimes a flavouring was added, such as honey or garlic.

The dough was left to rise and then put into clay moulds, or patted into shape, and baked in a mud brick oven.

Beer and Wine

Egyptian beer was made from barley. The barley was put into jars full of water and left to stand.

Then lightly baked bread was crumbled into the jars and the mixture was left to ferment.

The result was very thick and lumpy, so it had to be stirred and then passed through a sieve.

The beer was then poured into jars. A covering, possibly a leaf, was placed over the mouth of the jar, with a lump of mud on top as a stopper.

The beer in the jars was still a bit thick, so it was usually poured through a pottery strainer before being drunk.

Making wine

To make wine, the grapes were put into a large trough and men trampled up and down on them. The juice that came out was used to make the best wine.

The last drops of juice were squeezed from the grapes like this. The wine made from this juice was of a poorer quality.

The juice was poured into jars and left to ferment. Then the jars were sealed and labelled with the date and the name of the vineyard.

Sports

Wrestling was a popular sport. One tomb painting shows details of many of the holds and throws that were used.

Fencing may have begun as a sport for soldiers. A wooden sword was used and a narrow shield fastened to the left arm.

Hunting hippopotamus and crocodile could be both exciting and dangerous. People went out in boats with harpoons and ropes.

Nobles went out hunting animals in the desert. This was done on foot until the New Kingdom, when horses and chariots were often used

Boatmen sometimes held water tournaments. The object was to push your opponents into the water with a pole, before they pushed you.

A day on the river

The Egyptians spent a lot of their free time on the river. Some just went for boat trips or picnics. Others tried to spear fish or catch birds by throwing sticks. Noblemen often had

hunting cats, which were trained to find and bring back dead brids. Sometimes tame birds were held in the air to attract the other birds.

Children's Toys and Games

Brightly coloured leather balls have been found in the remains of Ancient Egyptian houses.

This Middle Kingdom tomb painting shows girls playing a game which involves throwing balls, while riding piggyback.

These children are playing a game rather like a tug of war. An Old Kingdom tomb painting shows several other, similar, energetic games.

Children played with spinning tops. A number of tops have been found in tombs.

Model animals made of mud, like these, may have been part of a farmyard game.

This ivory dog opens its mouth as if it were barking, when you press the lever in its chest.

By operating a handle at the side, you can make these ivory dwarfs twirl and dance.

Some dolls were made of wood and had moveable arms and legs.

This lion on wheels snaps its jaw as it moves along.

This basket containing a child's jewellery and charms was found in a little girl's grave.

25

Entertainments

Music was one of the most important forms of entertainment in Ancient Egypt. Professional singers and dancers performed in public during festivals and at private parties. No music was ever written down, though we know the words of some of the songs.

This tomb painting shows a typical group of musicians, with pipes, a lute and a harp.

Egyptian instruments also included flutes and lyres. Some, like this lyre, have survived in tombs.

Some noble households employed choirs of professional singers as permanent staff.

Most rich people were taught some musical skills as children. This noblewoman is playing to her husband.

As there was no written music, blind people, like this harpist, could easily become singers or musicians.

Dancing

Women dancers performed in processions at festivals. Some played tambourines or castanets to keep the beat. Young girls began training as dancers from an early age.

Tomb paintings show different styles of dances. This one appears to have been slow and graceful.

Others, like this one, were more lively and involved spectacular high kicks.

Some dancers hired for parties could also do acrobatics. This girl is turning a somersault.

The Egyptians probably enjoyed novelty acts too. This foreign slave girl is performing a dance from her country.

26

Indoor games

Senet was a popular board game, played rather like draughts.

Hounds and Jackals was probably also common, though we do not know how it was played.

Instead of dice, the Egyptians threw sticks or dried bones to decide how many moves could be made in a game.

An Egyptian party

Egyptian nobles had large parties with lots of food and drink. People often brought their pets – cats, dogs, monkeys and even geese. Singers, dancers, jugglers and acrobats were employed to entertain the guests. Servants served food and wine and offered people garlands of flowers and cones of perfumed grease to put on their heads.

Towns

Building land in towns was scarce, so many people lived in tall, narrow houses, several storeys high. They had no gardens, so they spent as much time as they could on their roofs, to catch the cool breeze. The streets were hot, dusty and noisy.

The market

Instead of shops, stalls were set up out of doors, selling locally produced fruit, vegetables and crafts.

Sometimes there was a stall selling beer, so that people could quench their thirsts in the heat.

Foreign Trade

Egypt was a great trading nation. Trade had been going on with neighbouring countries since Predynastic times. Although foreign trade was supposed to be controlled by the king, sailors would sometimes slip ashore to sell things privately.

From Syria and the Lebanon, Egypt imported wine, silver, slaves and horses. The Egyptians also imported Lebanese timber. This was important as few big trees grew in Egypt.

From the Nubian mines came an extra supply of gold for the Egyptians. They also imported Nubian copper, ivory, ostrich eggs and feathers, animal skins, amethysts, incense and slaves.

These people are Keftiu traders. They came from some islands in the Mediterranean Sea.

Wandering bedouin tribes came to Egypt from the desert to sell eye paints.

Cyprus exported copper, in pieces shaped like ox-hides, and opium, which was used as a medicine.

From Punt, which was somewhere in East Africa, the Egyptians brought back myrrh trees, which they used for making incense.

Here is an Egyptian boat being loaded with goods for export. The main exports were grain, papyrus, linen and rope.

People's Jobs

Most boys in Ancient Egypt followed the careers of their fathers. As soon as they were old enough, they followed their fathers into the fields or to a workshop where they learned a trade. Girls were generally expected to stay at home, helping their mothers, but there were some careers open to them. They could become musicians, dancers, professional mourners, weavers, bakers or midwives. They too began work at an early age.

Sculptors, carpenters, potters and other craftsmen usually worked together in workshops attached to a palace, temple or noble's house. There were a few who worked independently.

Potters

Egyptian potters mixed clay with finely chopped straw or sand, to bind it together. Men trampled up and down to mix it.

The pot was then shaped on a turntable, which the potter's assistant turned by hand.

The pots were baked in a wood-burning kiln. To prevent the pots from cracking, the fire had to be watched and the temperature kept even.

Carpenters

This is a set of carpenter's tools. They are made of copper and bronze with wooden handles.

Here are some carpenters at work. One man is polishing wood, the next is using a mallet and chisel. Another is shaping wood with a tool called an adze and the last is sawing.

Leatherworkers

Leather was used to make bags, sandals and many other things. These men are making arrow quivers.

Metalworkers

Here are some metalsmiths at work. Apprentices blow the fire to make it blaze fiercely. One man is pouring melted copper into a mould, while another is hammering a piece of cold copper into shape.

Royal tomb-builders

A good job to have in the New Kingdom was that of royal tomb-builder. The sixty men who worked on the royal tombs had their own village at Deir el Medineh, near the Valley of Kings. They were well treated, well paid and given plenty of free time.

There were slaves attached to the village to do the daily chores for them, such as chopping wood.

The men were divided into two teams, one for the right-hand side of the tomb, the other for the left. Each team had its own foreman.

Scribes kept a record of the progress of the work, the tools issued to workmen and the reasons for absence.

Wages were paid in goods, such as linen or food. Here a man is loading his wages on to a donkey.

We know from documents that sometimes the wages did not arrive and the men went on strike.

Boat-builders

Papyrus boats were made by tying bundles of reeds together. These boats were very light and were only used on the river, not on the sea.

To maked wooden boats, timbers were lashed and pegged together, so that, if necessary, they could be taken apart and rebuilt.

31

Temples

Along the banks of the Nile today you can see the remains of many temples. Most of them were built in the New Kingdom and later. Temples were dedicated to the worship of a particular god or goddess and contained a shrine with a statue, in which the god was supposed to live. Priests were in charge of looking after the god's daily needs.

The earliest temples, built in Predynastic times, were made of reeds and had flag-poles marking the entrance.

In the Old Kingdom, stone temples were built to honour the sun. A huge monument, a symbol of the sun god, stood in the courtyard.

This "kiosk" was built in the Middle Kingdom. This was where the god's shrine was taken during processions.

A New Kingdom temple

Temples were always built of stone and to the same basic design. They had an open courtyard, a hypostyle (pillared) hall and a holy of holies or sanctuary. People had to be specially purified before entering a temple. Only the king and priests could go beyond the courtyard.

Pylon or gateway

The capitals of the columns are shaped like plants.

Obelisk (monument to the sun god)

Statue of the king

Sphinxes

A morning service

There were three services each day, at sunrise, noon and sunset. Only the priests and priestesses, and occasionally the king and queen, attended. The morning service was to call the spirit of the god into his statue, and to offer him food, water, flowers and incense.

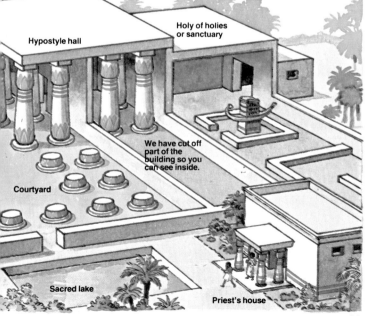

Hypostyle hall

Holy of holies or sanctuary

We have cut off part of the building so you can see inside.

Courtyard

Sacred lake

Priest's house

Religion in Daily Life

Scarab beetle

Ankh – sign of life

Djed

Wedjet – eye of the god Horus

Amulets were charms which everyone kept to protect them from danger or evil. You can find them in the designs on jewellery or furniture. Here are some of the most common.

People used spells to protect themselves against illness, accidents or devils. Here a mother is holding an ankh and saying a spell to protect her child.

This wall has been cut away so you can see behind it.

The king could approach a god at any time to question him. This was called taking an oracle. In answer, the god might speak or raise an arm. In fact, a priest was hiding behind the statue, speaking or operating it, as he felt the god wanted him to.

Ordinary people could not enter temples, so they dictated their questions to the priest who read them for them.

Sometimes you could take an oracle from a sacred animal, representing a god. The priests prayed to bring the god's spirit into the animal and interpreted its reactions to give you your answer.

To win favour with the gods, people went on pilgrimages to temples, or to holy places, such as Abydos, where the god Osiris died.

Sometimes people gave carvings of ears on stone as offerings, to remind the gods to listen to their prayers.

Anyone who wanted to find out the meaning of a strange dream could go to a priest, who would consult his books.

If a prayer was answered or an illness cured, people usually left a gift at the temple to thank the god.

Festivals

During great festivals people stopped work and went out on to the streets. The statue of the god in its shrine was placed on a boat and carried on poles through the streets.

People could approach and ask a question or favour. If the answer was "yes", the statue would suddenly become so heavy that the bearers went down on their knees.

As part of the festival, masked priests and priestesses performed plays re-enacting the stories of the gods.

People took food and other offerings to the tombs of their dead relations, who were supposed to come through the false door to share the feast.

Illness

If you were ill, as a last resort, you could go to a temple for a cure. You spent the night in a room near the sanctuary.

The god might appear in a dream to cure you. If the god didn't come, the priest would try to cure you the next day.

Black magic

Evil people practised black magic. This woman is sticking pins into a model of a man, hoping to kill him.

35

The King and Queen

The Egyptian king was called "pharaoh", which means "great house". Egypt had been ruled by two kings, one in the north (Lower Egypt) and one in the south (Upper Egypt). In 3118BC, the king of Upper Egypt conquered Lower Egypt and the country was united. The Egyptians believed their king was descended from the gods. He was High Priest of all the temples as well as head of the law and administration.

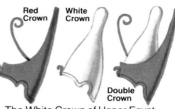

Red Crown   White Crown   Double Crown

The White Crown of Upper Egypt and the Red Crown of Lower Egypt were joined to make the Double Crown, worn by the king after unification.

On some carvings the unification of Egypt is shown by gods tying together papyrus and a lily – the symbols of the two lands.

The vulture goddess of the south and the snake goddess of the north are shown on the king's everyday head-dress.

Egyptians believed that at certain times the gods spoke through the king. This statue shows the king with the god Horus, shown as a falcon.

At the court

The king's daily duties included receiving advice and giving instructions to officials, architects and engineers, listening to petitions and receiving foreign ambassadors. Here a delegation of Libyans are paying their respects to the king and queen.

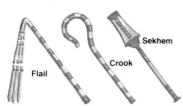

A sceptre is a symbol of a king's authority. In Egypt the most important were the Crook and Flail, but the king had others, such as the Sekhem (power) sceptre.

One of the king's roles was commander-in-chief of the army. New Kingdom kings were often great warriors and many led their troops into battle in person.

People paid taxes to the king in goods, such as grain, and services. The taxes paid for officials and workmen, and the care of the old and sick.

After a 30 year reign, a Heb Sed festival was held, to restore the king's health magically. During this, he ran along a special track.

Egyptians believed that when a king died he joined the god Osiris and ruled over the dead. This painting shows the king with Osiris.

The Queen

A king could have many wives but only one queen. She was usually the eldest daughter of the previous king and queen.

In the New Kingdom, the queen was also regarded as the wife of the god Amun. This made her the High Priestess.

If the king died while his eldest son was a child, the queen would become regent, ruling on behalf of the son.

Princes

In Ancient Egypt many children died young, so all the princes were trained carefully, in case they became king.

To become king, a prince had to marry the royal heiress, eldest daughter of the king and queen. This meant he had to marry his sister or half-sister. Here one of the minor wives is trying to introduce her son to the royal heiress.

37

The Government and Officials

The king governed with the help of his officials. These were often men who were related to the king, or who had been brought up with him. Others were ordinary men with distinguished careers in the army or as scribes in government service. The government was divided into departments of state – the Treasury, Foreign Affairs and Building. Each had a large staff, ranging from the chief official to the many scribes.

The most powerful official was the Vizier. His duties included reporting to the king each day on the state of the nation, giving orders to the various departments and collecting taxes.

Nomarchs, or governors, ruled the regions until the Middle Kingdom. Then they became too powerful and the king abolished them. This is the Nomarch Khnumhotep.

In the New Kingdom, a new official was created to govern the province of Nubia. He was called the "King's Son of Kush".

Some officials were sent on trading expeditions or put in charge of a mining project.

The king had a large staff of household servants and courtiers to attend on him.

The king's favourite courtiers and officials were called "fan bearers", after the emblem they carried. They always had easy access to the king.

If an official gave a beautiful daughter or sister to the king as a minor wife, this might win him favour.

A successful official could become wealthy, if the king honoured him with an award of gold.

Some people offered bribes to gain favours. Although officials were well paid, they sometimes accepted them.

Priests

Every temple had a High Priest and assistant priests of various ranks. To become priests, boys were trained in scripture and rituals. After a special ceremony, they were accepted into a particular temple, joining one of four groups of priests.

Each group was on duty in the temple for three months each year. Before going on duty, a priest had to be completely pure. His body was washed and shaved. He chewed natron – a kind of salt – and inhaled incense, to purify his mouth and thoughts.

All temples had priestesses too. Some could conduct religious services, but their main task was to sing hymns and make the responses to the prayers.

People paid taxes to the temple, to help support the priests. Sometimes disagreements arose over payment.

Priests were given different tasks. Some were in charge of the estates or workshops belonging to the temple.

Others specialized in performing funeral services or offering services to the dead.

Some priests studied the stars and the art of interpreting dreams.

"Wab" were men who never became full priests. They carried the shrine through the streets at festivals.

Musicians and dancers were attached to every temple and performed at most religious ceremonies.

Building

When the king wants to build a new temple the chief architect has to draw a plan and make a model for his approval.

Men begin quarrying stone from the cliffs. Using tools of stone, copper and wood, they drive lines of wooden wedges into the stone. Water is poured on to the wedges, to make them swell. As they swell, the slab of stone splits away from the rock face.

The stones are then dragged on sledges to the ships waiting to take them to the site of the new temple.

A lot of this work is done by men paying their labour tax to the king.

The king attends the foundation ceremony, in which the plan of the building is laid out with stakes and string.

The foundations are dug and the stone foundations are laid. Many of these workers are prisoners of war.

When the first layer of stone for the entire building has been laid, the areas between the stones are filled with sand.

A ramp of mud is built up alongside the first layer of stone, so that the second layer can be raised up more easily. After each layer of stone has been laid, the gap between the stones is filled with sand and the ramp made higher.

Once the roof has been completed, the ramps and sand are removed, so that you can get into the building.

Artists and sculptors

Before painting the wall of a tomb, Egyptian artists first made a grid of squares, to help them get the proportions of the drawing right. This was done with pieces of string soaked in paint.

Then a trainee artist drew in the required scene, taking care to follow the plan, which was drawn out on squares on a piece of papyrus. A master artist was there to supervise and make corrections.

Then the scenes were painted in, or carved and then painted.

Statues of gods, kings or private individuals were made for temples and tombs. The sculptors used tools made of copper and stone.
Sculptors and artists didn't sign their work.

Raising an obelisk

Obelisks, symbols of the sun god, stood outside temples. To erect an obelisk, ramps were built, with a hole in the middle filled with sand. The obelisk was pulled up the ramp backwards with ropes, then raised into position on top of the column of sand.

As the sand was removed from a hole in the bottom, the obelisk sank down slowly on to its base. Then the ramps were taken away.

Making mud bricks

Mud brick, rather than stone, was used for houses, palaces and government buildings. First large amounts of earth had to be dug.

The earth was mixed with water and straw, to help it bind together. This was done in a shallow pit by men stamping up and down.

When the mixture was ready, it was put into wooden moulds and left to dry in the sun.

41

The Army

In the Old Kingdom, men were drafted as soldiers by the local governors whenever they were needed. This system was abolished in the Middle Kingdom, as it had made the local governors too powerful and led to fighting between them. Gradually a royal army was built up. Some soldiers were full-time, others were drafted, probably as part of their tax duties to the king.

Until about 1600BC the army was made up of infantry, or foot soldiers, only. They carried spears, and shields of wood and leather.

Nubian archers were often hired to serve in the Egyptian army. Sometimes they had to fight in battles against their own people.

In the New Kingdom there were quite a few foreign recruits serving in special units of the army. They were people whose countries had been conquered by the Egyptians.

Fortresses

By the Middle Kingdom, the Egyptians had conquered part of Nubia. They built a chain of huge brick fortresses to protect this new southern frontier. Fortresses were also built along the eastern border, to keep out the bedouin tribes from the Sinai Desert.

Ships

The army used ships mainly for transporting troops. They fought very few sea battles.

Weapons

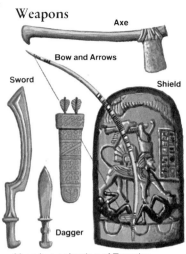

Here is a selection of Egyptian weapons. They were made of wood, stone, copper and bronze. Weapons belonging to kings or nobles often had rich inlays, like this shield belonging to Tutankhamun.

Sieges

For attacking enemy fortresses, the Egyptians had battering rams, with covers to protect the soldiers inside. Ladders were used to scale the walls. Some had wheels so that they could be pushed around.

Horses and chariots

In the New Kingdom there were four chariot squadrons in the army. Horses and chariots had been brought to Egypt by a people called the Hyksos, who conquered and ruled Egypt between 1670 and 1457BC. The chariots had two horses each and usually a driver as well as a warrior. Some soldiers did fight and drive, by tying the reins around their waists.

The Army on Campaign

In the New Kingdom the Egyptians believed that the god Amun directed the king to fight wars and conquer foreign lands. Here the king takes a sword from the statue of the god Amun.

This is a New Kingdom warrior ready for battle. His armour was made of leather, though it sometimes had metal scales. Some soldiers did other work during peacetime, so they had to be called up to fight.

On campaign the soldiers set up camps with tents. The officers had roomy, well-equipped tents with furniture, and servants.

This folding bed belonged to Tutankhamun. Officers probably had similar furniture in their tents.

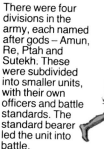

There were four divisions in the army, each named after gods – Amun, Re, Ptah and Sutekh. These were subdivided into smaller units, with their own officers and battle standards. The standard bearer led the unit into battle.

Trumpets were used to sound orders on the battlefield. This trumpet, and the wooden stopper which fits inside when the trumpet is being transported, belonged to Tutankhamun.

As a reward for courage, a soldier could be awarded a golden "fly" by the king. Archaeological finds show that some people received several.

After the battle

After a battle the right hands of all the dead enemies were cut off, to find out how many had been killed.

Chiefs who had led rebellions were sometimes executed. Pictures show the king doing this himself.

Prisoners of war were paraded before the god Amun. They became slaves of the king, the soldiers, or the temples.

Many prisoners of war ended up in the mines or on building projects, though some became household slaves.

The children of conquered princes were taken as hostages, to make sure their families remained loyal.

In a peace treaty the king often took the daughter of a foreign prince as one of his lesser wives.

Conquered peoples

The conquered land became part of the Egyptian Empire and its people had to pay regular tribute to Egypt. Here are Syrians presenting gifts of gold vases.

Messengers travelled regularly to all parts of the empire with instructions from the king and greetings for foreign kings.

Once conquered, the Nubians adopted the Egyptian gods and way of life. New towns were built, and temples, like this one at Abu Simbel.

In the eastern part of the empire, Egypt installed garrisons, took taxes and controlled foreign policy, but did not try to change the way of life, as they had done in Nubia.

Law

The police force was probably made up of soldiers. In the New Kingdom, in Thebes, a Nubian tribe called the Medjay were used as police, and as guards for the royal tombs.

It was difficult for criminals to escape from Egypt, as they had to cross deserts and go without water. The police used dogs to follow their trail.

The law courts

Most criminals were tried in local courts by a group of judges, who were important local men. There do not seem to have been any lawyers, so people were expected to conduct their own cases.

Witnesses had to swear by Amun and the king to tell the truth. If they refused to give evidence or were found to be lying, they were beaten.

In very difficult cases, where the judges could not reach a decision, they sometimes appealed to the oracle for help.

Punishments included beating, the loss of an ear or nose and hard labour, but there were no regular punishments for particular crimes.

Scribes were always in court, to take down the facts and examine documents produced as evidence at the trial.

Documents have survived which tell us about some thieves who were caught robbing the royal tombs in the Valley of the Kings. They were given the death sentence.

Appeals could be heard by the king or the Great Court, where important trials were held. One such case was the trial of the minor wives who tried to kill King Ramesses III.

Marriage

With the exception of the king, very few Egyptian men had more than one wife at a time. The women of Ancient Egypt were in a much better position than most other women in the Ancient World. Although they had little political power, they had personal freedom and independence.

Many marriages were arranged, though surviving poems suggest that young people also made their own choices.

On marriage, a husband and wife set up a joint fund to provide security for themselves and their children.

All married women had property of their own, and were allowed to dispose of it as they wished, without consulting their husbands.

A woman could take charge of running her estate herself and would manage her husband's business when he was away.

If a married woman had a job, she could spend her wages as she liked and was responsible for her own debts. This woman is spending her earnings on expensive jewellery, much to the dismay of her husband.

A man who ill-treated his wife was usually looked down upon. He might be beaten up or taken to court by her family, or his wife might divorce him.

If a man divorced his wife, she kept her personal property, her share of the marriage fund and her children, and was free to remarry.

Here a dying woman is dictating her will to a scribe. Although the marriage fund automatically went to the children, she could decide who her own property should go to.

Funerals and the Afterlife

A nobleman has just died, although his family had hired the best doctors to try to save him.

The embalmers take the body to their workshops, where the internal organs are removed and put in "canopic" jars.

The body is covered with natron (a salt) to dry and preserve it and then wrapped in linen. We call an embalmed body a "mummy".

The heart is replaced with a magic "heart-scarab". Amulets are put in the bandages, to protect the body.

A mask is put on the head. Priests assist at the embalming, wearing masks to represent the gods.

After 70 days the funeral is held. The procession crosses the river to collect the body from the workshop.

The funeral procession

The procession, which includes professional mourners, priests and priestesses, then goes to the tomb. The coffin is drawn on a sledge. Servants carry furniture and offerings for the tomb. Egyptians believed life after death would be like life on earth, so they filled the tomb with everything the dead person would need for his comfort.

At the tomb door the "opening of the mouth" ceremony is held. This was supposed to give the dead man control over his body again. Then there is a funeral feast.

The coffin is placed in the stone sarcophagus in the underground burial chamber. The furniture and other offerings are put there too.

Then the priests leave, sweeping away their footprints as they go. The underground tomb chamber is tightly sealed, so that no-one can enter.

The rooms above ground are left unsealed, so that the Ka, or spirit priests, can come in and leave food offerings for the dead man.

The afterlife

The Egyptians believed that, during the ceremonies, the dead man's spirit crossed the River of Death into the Next World.

Having been given a Book of the Dead, containing a map and spells, he could pass through gates guarded by serpents.

He then had to be able to assure a group of stern judges that he had not committed various crimes while he was alive.

Before Osiris, the god of the dead, the man's heart was weighed against the Feather of Truth. If the heart was heavier, it meant he had led a wicked life and was handed over to a monster.

A good person entered a happy land, where all his dead friends and relations greeted him warmly.

Tombs

The earliest graves were holes in the sand, with stones piled on top. Ordinary people were buried like this throughout Egyptian times.

In Dynastic times, nobles and kings began to be buried in "mastabas" – mud brick buildings with rooms inside.

By the 4th Dynasty, stone mastabas were being used by nobles. Some had chapels attached to them.

From the end of the Old Kingdom, nobles were also buried in tombs cut inside cliffs, which were decorated inside with scenes from daily life.

This kind of tomb was still being used in the New Kingdom, though some tombs, like the one above, had chapels with open courtyards.

This tomb is from the Late Period in Ancient Egypt. It looks rather like a very small temple.

Coffins

In early times, people who could afford it had wooden coffins. Other people were wrapped in mats.

An Old Kingdom noble was buried in a stone coffin called a sarcophagus. Some were decorated with carvings.

Many Middle Kingdom coffins were made of wood and brightly painted. They had "magic eyes" for the dead to see through.

Human-shaped coffins began to be used in the Middle Kingdom. The coffins were then placed in outer, rectangular coffins of wood or stone. This one belonged to King Tutankhamun

This decorated wooden coffin and heavy stone sarcophagus come from the Late Period.

Pyramids and royal tombs

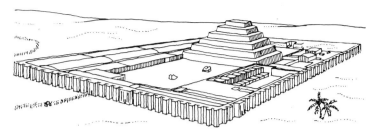

In the Old Kingdom, kings were buried in pyramids. the earliest ones are called "step" pyramids, as they were built in steps. The Egyptians believed that the king climbed up the pyramid to the stars. The first one, which is shown above, was built for King Zoser at Sakkara.

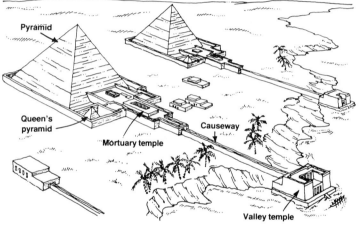

At the beginning of the 4th Dynasty, step pyramids were being replaced by "true" pyramids, like these. There was a collection of buildings around them. The embalming was done in the valley temple. Offerings to the dead king were made daily in the mortuary temple.

12th Dynasty pyramids were built of mud brick with a stone casing, instead of all stone. They lost their shape once the stone wore off.

In the New Kingdom, kings were buried in tombs cut into the rock in the Valley of Kings, at Thebes. Treasure was buried with them and the tombs were often attacked by robbers.

Writing

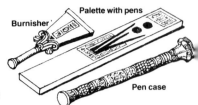

Burnisher

Palette with pens

Pen case

The Egyptians made written records of all business and legal matters, but as many people in Egypt could not read or write, scribes were specially employed to do this.

This is a scribe's writing equipment – a palette with pens, a pen case and a burnisher for smoothing down papyrus, a kind of paper made from papyrus reeds.

First the reeds were gathered and the outer green skin peeled away (left). The inner part was cut into strips and soaked in water (centre). Then the strips were placed, just overlapping, to make a sheet, with a layer of strips going the other way on top (right). The sheet was then pressed, dried and rolled.

Hieroglyphs

The Egyptians used a picture writing called hieroglyphs. At first, pictures were used just to represent objects. Later, the system developed and pictures and signs were used to represent sounds. Some sounds were for one letter, others were for groups of up to five letters. Words were built up of several different signs. Sometimes there was a picture of the object or action at the end of the word, to make it clearer what the word meant.

Hieratic

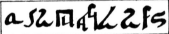

Hieroglyphic

Hieroglyphs were always used on monuments, but there were two shorthand scripts invented for everyday use. The one shown above is called hieratic.

Some hieroglyphs

OWL M	MOUTH R	WATER N	QUAIL CHICK W	LOAF T	BOLT S

FLAX H	FACE HR	SANDAL STRAP ANKH	GOOSE SA	SWALLOW WR	BEETLE KHEPER

You can always recognize a king's name, as it is written in an oval frame, called a cartouche.

Education and Science

Most Egyptian children didn't go to school. Instead boys were taught a trade by their fathers, as soon as they were old enough, while girls helped their mothers. Those who could afford it sent their sons to school or employed private tutors. Girls from rich families were taught to write too.

At school the children were taught to read and write. They spent much of the day copying texts or doing dictations. Rich or clever pupils sometimes went on to study history, maths, religion, geography and languages too.

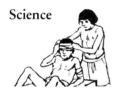

For notes and exercises, ostraca were used instead of papyrus. These were pieces of stone or broken pot.

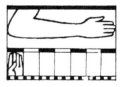

Boys who had received a good education might become one of the king's officials. Languages were important for anyone dealing with foreign affairs or trade.

Science

Egyptian doctors were famous for their knowledge and skill. Surviving texts give details of medicines and treatments.

This papyrus sets out sums involving triangles. Texts like this show that Egyptian scholars were good mathematicians.

Their measurements were based on the body. Elbow to fingertip was one cubit. Seven hands, each four fingers wide, also equalled one cubit.

Egyptians studied the positions of the stars, which they named after animals and gods. This is a map of the skies.

| 10 days = 1 week |
| 30 days = 1 month |
| 4 months = 1 season |
| 3 seasons = 1 year |
| 360 days + 5 days = 1 year |

This is the Egyptian calendar. Years were numbered from the beginning of the reign of each king.

Water hole

The day was divided into 24 hours. This is a water clock. You could tell the time by the water level as the water dripped through a hole.

Gods and Goddesses

Before Egypt was united, each region had its own gods and legends, so after the unification there were many gods – some local, some common to all Egypt. Most gods were associated with a particular animal, and they are often shown with the head or body of that animal. The Egyptians believed the gods ruled everything in nature, including the sun and sky.

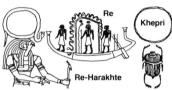

The sun god was one of the most important gods. The Egyptians had many versions of the sun god, but **Re** was the most common.

There were various stories about how the world began. One story is that it began with water. Then land appeared with a lotus flower on it. The flower opened and out of it came **Re**, who created the world.

In Memphis people said that their god **Ptah** created the world by saying the name of each thing, and so bringing it to life. His wife, **Sekhmet**, was goddess of war.

The body of the sky goddess, **Nut**, stretched from horizon to horizon. Her father **Shu**, god of air, stood over her brother **Geb**, god of earth, to hold her up.

In the New Kingdom, the god Amun was identified with Re and became **Amun-Re**, king of the gods.

Thoth was god of wisdom and scribes and helped judge the dead. Symbol: Ibis bird.

Maat. Goddess of truth. She kept the universe in harmony. Symbol: feather.

Khumn. Potter god who made babies. Symbol: ram.

Bast. Mother goddess, worshipped in the Late Period. Symbol: cat.

Sobek. God of water. Worshipped by many people because they feared him. Symbol: crocodile.

The story of Osiris

Osiris was the great-grandson of Re and god of the dead. He married his sister, the goddess **Isis**, and they became two of the most popular and influential gods. People believed they had once ruled Egypt, as king and queen. Here is a story associated with them.

Their brother **Set**, god of deserts, storms and war, was jealous. He murdered Osiris and cut his body into pieces.

The god **Horus**, son of Isis and Osiris, fought and defeated Set, who was diguised as a hippopotamus.

Anubis, the god of embalming, helped to collect the pieces of Osiris's body and bring him back to life.

Horus's wife, **Hathor**, was goddess of music, dancing and happiness. She also cared for the dead. Symbol: cow.

Household gods

Some gods were not worshipped in temples, but by ordinary people in their houses. **Bes**, the dwarf, was god of marriage and children. **Taweret**, who is shown as a hippopotamus, was goddess of pregnant women.

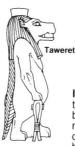

Imhotep, architect of the first stone pyramid, became god of medicine. He was the only commoner ever to become a god.

Sacred animals

Some temples kept an animal, as it was believed that the god's spirit could enter into it. A bull, known as the **Apis bull**, was always kept in Memphis. It was seen as the spirit of Ptah and buried as a king.

In the Late Period, whole species of animals were worshipped and buried with honour. This is a mummified cat.

Travel and Transport

It was useless to build roads in Egypt, as they would have been covered and washed away by the floods every year. So instead, people nearly always travelled by boat, with the Nile as Egypt's highway. This affected the Egyptian way of looking at things. Their words for north and south were "downstream" and "upstream". They also believed there was a river like the Nile in the sky, and every day the sun god sailed in a boat from one side of the world to the other.

Foreign trading vessels

Local cargo boat

Noble in private boat on official business.

Local ferry taking people from one side of the river to the other.

The earliest boats were made of reeds. These were used on the river throughout Ancient Egyptian times. as there was a shortage of good timber for boat-building.

By about 3200BC, wooden boats were in use. The wood was imported from the Lebanon, which had excellent timber. All sea-going ships were made of wood.

All heavy cargo went by river. Obelisks were taken on barges from the quarries to the temples, towed by smaller boats. During the floods the river became wider, so boats could travel further inland.

This is a funeral barge, used by embalmers to carry corpses across the river to their workshops on the west bank.

The royal family travelled around on splendidly decorated ships. This is what the Royal Ship of Tutankhamun may have looked like.

Travel on land

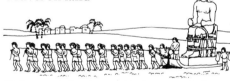

Statues and other heavy objects were pulled on sledges by teams of men with ropes. Water or oil was poured on the ground in front of the sledge, to help it run smoothly.

Traders used donkeys to transport things across the desert. Camels were not used until the Late Period.

To get around on land most people had to walk. Some very rich people were carried by their servants in chairs like these. Donkeys could be used for longer journeys.

Once chariots had been introduced in Egypt, noblemen could travel much faster. However most people could not afford horses and chariots.

A Map of Ancient Egypt

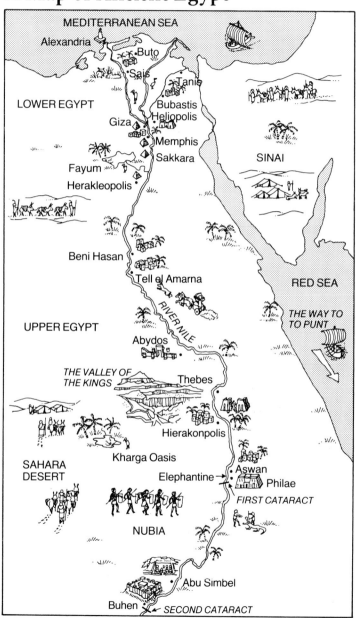

MEDITERRANEAN SEA

Alexandria

Buto

Sais

Tanis

LOWER EGYPT

Bubastis
Heliopolis

Giza

Memphis

Sakkara

Fayum

Herakleopolis

SINAI

Beni Hasan

Tell el Amarna

RED SEA

RIVER NILE

UPPER EGYPT

THE WAY TO
TO PUNT

Abydos

THE VALLEY OF
THE KINGS

Thebes

Hierakonpolis

Kharga Oasis

SAHARA
DESERT

Elephantine →

Aswan

Philae

FIRST CATARACT

NUBIA

Abu Simbel

Buhen

SECOND CATARACT

The History of Ancient Egypt

Thousands of years ago, Stone Age hunters lived in the Nile Valley. They have left behind remains, such as flint tools.

Predynastic Period

Later the hunters learned to tame animals and farm the land. The first farmers we know of were a group in Upper Egypt called Badarians. They made red pottery with black tops. Next came the Amratians, who made decorated pots, often with animal designs on them. After them were the Gerzeans. During this period, writing was invented and Egypt was divided into two kingdoms. These early cultures are named after the places where their remains were found.

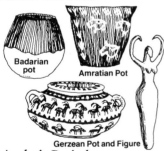

Badarian pot

Amratian Pot

Gerzean Pot and Figure

Archaic Period

In 3118BC, Menes, King of Upper Egypt, conquered Lower Egypt and so united the country. He became the first king of United Egypt, and of the 1st Dynasty. A new capital city was built at Memphis and a graveyard at Sakkara.

Old Kingdom

The period known as the Old Kingdom began with the 3rd Dynasty. It was a time of peace and prosperity, with no invasions from abroad. This was the time when the great pyramids were build. The first was the "step" pyramid at Sakkara, designed by the architect Imhotep for King Zoser.

The pharaohs of the 4th Dynasty built their pyramids to a different design. They are called "true" pyramids and the most famous are at Giza.

It was an age of great achievement in art, especially sculpture. These statues are of Prince Rahotep and his wife, Nofret.

1st Intermediate Period

Then came a troubled period. The nobles grew more powerful and the pharaohs lost their influence. Wars took place between local governors wanting to gain power.

Middle Kingdom

The wars came to an end when Mentuhotep, a prince of Thebes, seized power and reunited the land. This second period of peace and prosperity is called the Middle Kingdom. A magnificent tomb was built for King Mentuhotep at Thebes.

The 12th Dynasty kings had a new capital city built near the Fayum, a marshy piece of land which they had drained. Northern Nubia was conquered and a chain of fortresses was built to protect Egypt's new southern frontier from attack.

A lot of beautiful jewellery, such as this princess's crown, was made in the Middle Kingdom.

2nd Intermediate Period

Royal power declined once again and the country was torn by civil war. Egypt was invaded from the east by a people called the Hyksos, who ruled the country for over a hundred years. They brought the horse and chariot to Egypt. Finally a prince of Thebes led a revolt and expelled them.

New Kingdom

The New Kingdom began after the expulsion of the Hyksos. During this period, the Egyptians conquered a vast empire, which they ruled from the new capital, Thebes. The dotted line on the map shows the furthest extent of their empire.

Between 1503 and 1482BC Egypt was ruled by a woman pharaoh, Queen Hatshepsut, who seized power at the death of her husband. She was succeeded by her nephew, Tuthmosis III (1504–1425). He was a great warrior and much of Egypt's empire was won during his reign.

A later king, Amenophis IV (1379–1362), decided to abolish all the gods except one, Aten, the sun's disc. He changed his name to Akhenaten and made everyone worship Aten. He and his wife, Nefertiti, had a new capital built, at Amarna.

These changes were unpopular, so the next king, Tutankhamun (1361–1352), brought back the old gods and moved the capital back to Thebes.

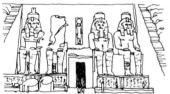

Egypt's enemies had grown stronger during Akhenaten's reign. Ramesses II (1304–1237) helped to restore the country's prestige. He was responsible for the building of the temple at Abu Simbel in Nubia.

Ramesses III (1198–1166) was Egypt's last great warrior king. He helped defend the country from invasion, by fighting a battle with a people from the Mediterranean islands, who were known as the "Sea Peoples".

3rd Intermediate Period

After this, Egypt began to decline. It was attacked by many invaders and many of the royal tombs were robbed. The empire was lost. For a hundred years a Nubian family ruled Egypt, as the 25th Dynasty. Then, in 664BC, Thebes was overrun by the Assyrians.

Late Period

In 664BC, the Prince of Sais drove out the Assyrians and later united Egypt under the 26th Dynasty. But in 525BC the Persians conquered Egypt and made it part of the Persian Empire.

The Persians were much hated and when Alexander the Great conquered Egypt in 332BC, he was welcomed by the Egyptians.

Ptolemaic Period

When Alexander died, his general, Ptolemy, founded a new dynasty of kings (the 31st and last), who ruled Egypt from the new city of Alexandria.

Roman Conquest

The last Ptolemy, Cleopatra, and her Roman husband, Mark Anthony, committed suicide after being defeated by the Romans. Egypt then became a Roman province.

Museums

Here are the names of museums where you can find exhibits from Ancient Egypt.

Australia

National Gallery of Victoria, **Melbourne**
Australian Museum, **Sydney**
Nicholson Museum of Australia, **Sydney**

Canada

Ethnological Museum, McGill University, **Montreal**
Museum of Fine Arts, **Montreal**
Royal Ontario Museum, **Toronto**

United Kingdom

City Museum, **Bristol**
Fitzwilliam Museum, **Cambridge**
Museum and Art Gallery, **Dundee**
Gulbenkian Museum of Oriental Art and Archaeology, **Durham**
Royal Scottish Museum, **Edinburgh**
Art Gallery and Museum, **Glasgow**
Burrell Collection, **Glasgow**
Hunterian Museum, **Glasgow**
Museum and Art Gallery, **Leicester**
Merseyside County Museum, **Liverpool**
School of Archaeology and Oriental Studies, **Liverpool**
British Museum, **London**
Horniman Museum, **London**
Victoria and Albert Museum, **London**
University Museum, **Manchester**
Castle Museum, **Norwich**
Ashmolean Museum, **Oxford**
Pitt Rivers Museum, **Oxford**

United States

Walters Art Gallery, **Baltimore,** Maryland
Robert H. Lowie Museum of Anthropology, **Berkeley,** California
Museum of Fine Arts, **Boston,** Massachusetts
Brooklyn Museum, **Brooklyn,** New York
Fogg Art Museum, Harvard University, **Cambridge,** Massachusetts
Semitic Museum, Harvard University, **Cambridge,** Massachusetts
Field Museum of Natural History, **Chicago,** Illinois
Oriental Institute Museum, **Chicago,** Illinois
Art Museum, **Cincinnati,** Ohio
Museum of Art, **Cleveland,** Ohio
Art Museum, **Denver,** Colorado
Detroit Institute of Arts, **Detroit,** Michigan
William Rockhill Nelson Gallery of Art, **Kansas City,** Missouri
County Museum of Art, **Los Angeles,** California
Institute of Arts Museum, **Minneapolis,** Minnesota
Yale University Art Gallery, **New Haven,** Connecticutt
Metropolitan Museum of Art, **New York**
Stanford University Museum, **Palo Alto,** California
Pennsylvania University Museum, **Philadelphia,** Pennsylvania
Museum of Art, Carnegie Institute, **Pittsburgh,** Pennsylvania
University Art Museum, **Princeton,** New Jersey
Rhode Island School of Design, **Providence,** Rhode Island
Museum of Fine Arts, **Richmond,** Virginia
Art Museum, **St Louis,** Missouri
Museum of Man, **San Diego,** California
M.H. De Young Memorial Museum, **San Francisco,** California
Rosicrucian Museum, **San José,** California
Art Museum, **Seattle,** Washington
Museum of Art, **Toledo,** Ohio
Smithsonian Institution, **Washington D.C.**
Art Museum, **Worcester,** Massachusetts

Index